SEASONS WILL CHANGE

SEASONS WILL CHANGE

A Taoist Approach to Teacher Wellbeing

MARIA WHITE

© **Copyright 2020 Maria White**
All rights reserved. Without limiting the rights under copyright reserved above, no part of this publication may be reproduced, stored in or introduced into a retrieval system, or transmitted, in any form or by any means (electronic, mechanical, photocopying, recording or otherwise), without the prior written permission of the copyright owner.

Disclaimer: The author does not provide medical advice or prescribe the use of any technique as a form of treatment for physical, emotional or medical problems without the advice of a physician, either directly or indirectly. The intent of the author is only to offer information to help you reclaim your presence as the 'The Master Teacher'. In the event you use any of the information in this book for yourself, the author and the publisher assume no responsibility.

Publishing Details:

A catalogue record for this book is available from the National Library of Australia

ISBN: 978-0-6487572-0-7 (Paperback)
ISBN: 978-0-6487572-1-4 (Ebook)

Cover and Interior Layout : Pickawoowoo Publishing Group
Cover photo: Markus Spiske (Unsplash)

Printing and channel distribution: Lightning Source / Ingram

TABLE OF CONTENTS

Acknowledgements · ix
Introduction· xi

Verse 1· ·1
Verse 2· ·2
Verse 3· ·3
Verse 4· ·4
Verse 5· ·5
Verse 6· ·6
Verse 7· ·7
Verse 8· ·8
Verse 9· ·9
Verse 10· ·10
Verse 11· ·11
Verse 12· ·12
Verse 13· ·13
Verse 14· ·14
Verse 15· ·15
Verse 16· ·16
Verse 17· ·17

Verse 18	18
Verse 19	19
Verse 20	20
Verse 21	21
Verse 22	22
Verse 23	23
Verse 24	24
Verse 25	25
Verse 26	26
Verse 27	27
Verse 28	28
Verse 29	29
Verse 30	30
Verse 31	31
Verse 32	32
Verse 33	33
Verse 34	34
Verse 35	35
Verse 36	36
Verse 37	37
Verse 38	38
Verse 39	40
Verse 40	41
Verse 41	42
Verse 42	43
Verse 43	44
Verse 44	45
Verse 45	46
Verse 46	47
Verse 47	48

Verse 48	49
Verse 49	50
Verse 50	51
Verse 51	52
Verse 52	53
Verse 53	54
Verse 54	55
Verse 55	56
Verse 56	57
Verse 57	58
Verse 58	59
Verse 59	60
Verse 60	61
Verse 61	62
Verse 62	63
Verse 63	64
Verse 64	65
Verse 65	66
Verse 66	67
Verse 67	68
Verse 68	69
Verse 69	70
Verse 70	71
Verse 71	72
Verse 72	73
Verse 73	74
Verse 74	75
Verse 75	76
Verse 76	77
Verse 77	78

Verse 78 · 80
Verse 79 ·81
Verse 80 ·82
Verse 81 · 83

ACKNOWLEDGEMENTS

Not having formally studied the *Tao Te Ching*, it should be noted that these verses are not an attempt at a direct translation. Primarily because I had originally compiled these verses for my own wellbeing, my referencing to the sage-like figure who appears in the *Tao* is female. But as Stephen Mitchell in his edition writes, "The Chinese language doesn't make this kind of distinction; in English we have to choose".

I used as inspiration the following translations for which I owe a great deal of thanks for the authors. Their dedication to communicating Lao-Tzu's messages helped me in writing this contextualised version for teachers.

For anyone interested in reading more about Lao-Tzu or the *Tao Te Ching*, I suggest reading through Mitchell's Introduction to his version of the text.

The Complete Tao Te Ching, translated by Gia-Fu Feng and Jane English, Vintage Books, 1972

Tao Te Ching: The Book of the Way by Lao Tzu, translated by Stephen Mitchell, Kyle Books, 2011

Tao Te Ching by Lao Tzu, translated by John H. McDonald, Chartwell Books, 2009

Headless Tao, Jim Clatfelder, The Shollond Trust, 2015

Getting Right with Tao: A Contemporary Spin on the Tao Te Ching, by Ron Hogan, Channel V Books, 2010

INTRODUCTION

To say that I am an expert at Taoism or the *Tao Te Ching* would be a gross understatement. Having been brought up Christian, I was always spiritually inclined, but by the time I became an adult I found myself somewhat disillusioned by the constrictive nature of institutionalised religion. Interestingly, in hindsight, my decline in adopting any form of faith in my 20s, also coincided with a steady rise in stress so profound that it resulted, by the time I was 28, in a significant mental breakdown which saw me pretty much unable to teach for three full months.

Faith, I have since found, has become a tainted word in our modern society, one associated with 'ignorant' religious beliefs. Yet faith is a concept which permeates every segment of our lives. We have to trust that our children will find their way as adults; that we will return by the end of the working day safe and sound; that the seasons will change. Our propensity to plan for futures without knowing for sure if they will pass, is indicative of our human capacity to believe and trust in the Universe – that it will go on. It is almost as if it is written our DNA.

My attempt at contextualising such an ancient text as the *Tao Te Ching* for the modern teacher and classroom may be ambitious at best. But I am a successful product of my belief in the teachings written here. As a seasoned teacher, I have clawed my way back into a vocation that

I love after being told, at my lowest, that teaching might not be for everyone and that perhaps I should consider something else. Deep in my gut, I inherently knew that this comment was wrong. For it is not that teaching that is not right for everyone, I have since discovered, but the ability to <u>become</u> the teacher, which mystifies many.

This little book of verses is just the first step I plan to take in helping fellow educators reclaim their presence as the Maestro, or in the case of this book, The Master Teacher. To help them regain not only faith in themselves, but to rightfully demand it of others. Although I am statistically one of the few who managed to return to teaching, it still saddens me to hear of yet another teacher who has left the industry for good. For I know that the adult in this situation will recover somehow and find their own way forward, but it is the child who is left behind who is ultimately the victim of this system.

And so I end with this:

For those educators who are struggling right now, know that you are not alone. You are not a failure. You are a teacher to the very core of your being, regardless of whether it is in a formal classroom or not. For you teach what it is to be human – a human *being*. And that is the greatest lesson you could ever teach anyone.

Maria White
The Mind Full Teacher

VERSE 1

There are a few different translations for the word Tao, such as The Way or How.
The Tao is a principle, a way of seeing how the world works.
It is eternal, as it relates to the creation of all things.
It cannot be defined, but it is real.
It can be found inside you, through self-awareness or meditation.

To discover it, a Master Teacher must adopt an open mind, and avoid prejudices.
A closed mind only sees what it wants to see.
By knowing about the Way, you know How things happen.

VERSE 2

In a balanced world, there are polarities.
When you recognise something as good, you immediately define what is bad.
As soon as you define what 'is', its opposite must be true.
Up needs down.
High needs low.
Light needs dark.
Easy needs hard.

Finding true balance is challenging.
If you focus too much on one side of the spectrum, the other side will eventually appear.
A person obsessed with beauty, over time becomes ugly.
A person who brags about being charitable, is in the end egotistical.

Therefore a Master Teacher should try to let events unfold naturally,
Rather than push them.
She should let pressures come and go,
Without fixating on them.
She should work well and passionately,
Without expecting praise in return.
A Master Teacher knows that leading by example is the most effective way,
And that is why she is so well respected.

VERSE 3

By praising one behaviour too much,
A teacher disregards other behaviours.
Students will therefore strive to please the teacher,
Rather than respect other ways of being,
And so will start judging their own performance.

If a teacher becomes materialistic,
And focuses too much on grades and outcomes,
They create a climate of competitiveness,
And students will no longer take risks for fear of failure.

A Master Teacher understands
That her role is to disrupt, not accelerate, a child's conditioning.
To raise questions,
And challenge a student's understanding of the world.
To get them out of their heads,
And into their hearts.
Then to stand back and watch what unfolds.

VERSE 4

The Tao is a principle, rather than a process or thing,
Therefore it is without limits.
It creates, but does not take.
It explains all behaviours and events,
And is forever present.

VERSE 5

Those who know of the Tao
Understand that in a balanced world,
The justice handed down by Nature will take no sides.
Consequences for actions will unfold in equal measure.

The Master Teacher will therefore accept every student
and colleague,
And will not judge them.
No one person is better than another.
Every deed will see an equal response.
She appreciates that this principle applies to all – including her –
So she will strive, herself, to stay centred and balanced.

VERSE 6

The Tao is eternal because it is the natural order of things.
To live the Tao is to be open minded and open hearted.
To accept all with good faith and good will.

You can feel the Tao in quiet contemplation and meditation.
The Tao is always in you and around you.
When you look upon the world, you also look upon the Tao.
Like the wind, you cannot see it,
But you can see what it creates.

VERSE 7

The Tao is eternal, because it never ceases to be.
It is not of the ego, because it has no self.
Yet it is present in everything.

Thus the Master Teacher understands that when she gives,
She should do so without the ego in mind.
She must learn to detach herself, in order to become attached.
Must avoid becoming a follower, in order to lead.
Must let go of desire, in order to inspire.

The Master Teacher feels true self-fulfilment
Once she stops striving to fulfil the self.
This is the great paradox.

VERSE 8

True goodness is like water:
It flows steadily down through every crevice and every niche.
It nourishes and refreshes,
It cleans and gives life.
It does not judge.
It is content.
It just is.

The Master Teacher attempts to live in the same way:
Her presence is gentle but persistent and her impact, profound.
She feeds thirsty minds.
Her influence lifts others.
She is kind and honest.
She is at ease.
She is present.

A Master Teacher does not force, but is fluid like water.
She has no need to push, so now no-one need yield.
Students will no longer feel defensive nor resentful,
Thus everyone will respect her leadership.

VERSE 9

Teachers seeking perfection,
Will never be accepting of imperfections.
Teachers who concentrate on building careers,
Stop concentrating on building connections.
If your mindset is on the chase,
Then you will never finish the race.

Master Teachers do not seek approval nor fame from others.
They focus on doing good work and letting it speak for itself.
Therefore a Master Teacher knows when a job is completed,
And when to confidently step back, relax and let events unfold.

VERSE 10

Can you stay focused on your reasons for teaching
When all around you others complain and critique?

Can you maintain a positive and flexible approach
When changes occur with little warning?

Can you stop yourself from looking back,
Using it as an excuse from moving forward?

Can you learn to teach others
Without making it about your feelings?

Give and nurture selflessly.
Your impact on others may not reveal itself immediately.
In fact, you may never see it.
So do not invest so much in outcomes.
Have faith in your power and your presence.

VERSE 11

A teacher focuses on the number of students in a classroom.
A Master Teacher focuses on the atmosphere contained within it.
She may have 10 or thirty in a class; its size is of no concern to her.
What matters is not in what is seen, but what is felt.

When a vase is formed, it is the space created within which makes it useful.
When a room is built, its walls are not as important as its liveable space inside.
Thus a Master Teacher learns to concentrate more on the silences and empty spaces,
Rather than what is being said or done.
This is where her true insight lies.

VERSE 12

Excessiveness can drive people mad.
The same applies to your senses.
Too much noise can be deafening.
Too much brightness, blinding.

A Master Teacher understands that a balanced classroom means
Allowing time for stillness and contemplation.
She teaches students to know when the time is right
To stop and let go of trivialities.
She teaches them to focus their senses on simple sensations instead,
By modelling the process herself.

VERSE 13

A Master Teacher does not look for praise from others.
Seeking success is just as dangerous as failing.
Teachers who become dependent upon the opinions of others,
Learn to rely on them rather than their own personal development.

Confidence comes from working well and to the best of your ability,
But confidence is lost the greater your reputation grows.
Autonomy can be powerful.
But power can restrict freedom.

A Master Teacher stays grounded by fostering self-compassion.
To be able to teach well, she must be in fine health.
A Master Teacher accepts who she is and values her place in
the world,
Thus loses any sense of anxiety or worry.

Caring for the self is not self-ish, caring for the self is self-less.
When there is less self, there is less ego,
So she is able to be both successful and humble.

VERSE 14

When confronted by a situation,
Or a conversation you are failing to understand,
Learn to stand back and be still in the moment.
For the harder you try to look, the less you will see clearly.
The harder you try to listen, the less you will actually hear.
The harder you try to control it, the less affect you will have.

A Master Teacher has learnt to try less, in order to succeed more.
To approach challenges with openness, in order to discover more.
To be calm and silent, in order to hear more.

When she listens, she becomes influential.
When she is detached, she becomes wise.

VERSE 15

Eminent teachers from the past knew and understood the world,
But never sought to tame or control it.

Those teachers were observant but alert.
Courteous yet subtle and fluid in nature.
Simple in appearance but profound in thought.
Open and transparent in both their hearts and minds.

Ask yourself if you can be that patient.
Can you be still until the drama dissipates,
And wait for the right move to reveal itself?

A Master Teacher does not do her work for glory.
She does not lead by promoting herself,
Or by reacting too swiftly to changing whims.
She is calm, present and receptive to all things.

VERSE 16

A Master Teacher learns to meditate or spend time reflecting,
In order to feel inner peace.
A Master Teacher learns to observe the natural world around her,
So remembers that all things will return to their original state.

We have all come from nothing, and will return to nothing.
Nothingness is stillness. Nothingness is peace.

A teacher who forgets the bigger picture,
Stresses too much on the finer details.
A teacher who ignores the constant and consistent force of Nature,
Mistakenly believes that she can control it.
A Master Teacher is calm and tolerant and slightly amused,
As she remembers where she comes from and where she's going to.
She is serene, and lives with no remorse.

No matter the challenge faced, nor the obstacle ahead,
Being reminded of the Tao – the How – is a source of
immediate relief.

VERSE 17

A Master Teacher leads without making students feel lead.
The next best teacher is respected as they are well liked.
Then there are those who are obeyed through discipline.
And worst, there are those who are hated and despised.

The Master Teacher teaches to a child's higher self,
And places trust in their potential to reach it.

The Master Teacher does not tell, but shows.
Guides rather than orders.
A Master Teacher's job is done,
When their students can exclaim
That they did it all by themselves.

VERSE 18

When students forget to be good,
Start talking about kindness and charity.

When students forget their humanity,
Focus on rebuilding compassion.

When students question what is authentic,
Point out self-evident truths.

When students stop being respectful,
Emphasise politeness.

When a class becomes confused and disordered,
Place attention on loyalty and trust.

VERSE 19

If you were to stop stressing the teaching of content,
Your students would learn more.
If you were to stop threatening with rules and punishments,
Your students would be more kind and respectful.
If you were to stop making grades the sign of achievement,
Your students would be more successful.

Stop addressing the superficial.
These are projections of other people's desires.
Teaching to a child's potential is more powerful.

VERSE 20

Trying to control everything,
Is the source of all your worries.
Why should you care how others judge you?
Whether you're a success or failure?
Why be anxious about what others think?

Seeking approval from others,
Being concerned about their opinions,
Will only ever leave you feeling fear.

Let others act in a whimsical fashion.
What makes them happy changes from one day to the next.
Let others be ambitious and driven.
They love the chase rather than the end result.
Let others think that they are cleverer than you,
They believe there is no more learning to be done.

Master Teachers may at times feel isolated,
Or misunderstood.
They alone have gone against the crowd.
They know they are different.
For to truly live with the Tao in mind,
Means understanding that no one is actually in control.

VERSE 21

You can recognise a Master Teacher
By their luminous glow.

You cannot define it, you cannot grasp it.
Their personalities appear open yet profound.
They appear both centred and still.
Yielding, yet unable to be swayed.

For they have learnt to focus inward,
Rather than outward.
They choose to stay connected with the Tao.

VERSE 22

If you wish your students to advance,
Then learn to step away.
If you wish to be respected by them,
Then show vulnerability.
If you wish for them to find an answer,
Then admit that you don't know everything.

A Master Teacher who lives by the Tao,
Teaches through example.
Becomes influential,
By avoiding power.
Is not boastful nor arrogant,
So students believe her.
Is so grounded and self-assured,
That students trust her.
Is so giving and selfless,
That students don't fight her.

There is truth in the saying,
That you are at your strongest,
When you are at your weakest.
When you are authentic,
Authenticity shows up in your life.

VERSE 23

Do not forbid the expression of any emotion.
Allow them all to be voiced.
For just like in Nature, a storm will never last forever.
The rain will pass,
The wind will slow,
The animals will re-emerge,
And the sun will shine again.

A Master Teacher knows that to deny any emotion,
Is to place down blocks of resistance.
Which, like an ill built dam,
Will eventually crumble under the pressure of the river,
And flood the plain below.

To be reminded of the Tao,
Is to be reminded that in a balanced world,
Binaries are necessary.
Place trust in why every emotion must exist,
And others will learn to trust them too.

VERSE 24

A Master Teacher is like a great tree.
Her trunk is grounded and balanced,
With roots firmly planted in the ground.
Her branches are pliable and resilient,
Against sudden winds of change.
Her leaves grow to provide shade in summer,
And withdraw to allow the sun in through in winter.
She has no need to brag nor boast,
Her very presence speaks volumes to others.

The Master Teacher has no need for excesses,
Does not spend time comparing herself to others.
She knows who she is.
She has a purpose and works towards it,
Creating an enduring legacy.

VERSE 25

In some way, by some circumstance,
Our world, our universe, was formed.
Some see it as spiritual,
Some see it as scientific.
I do not know its cause.
But I do call it the Tao.
The Way or the How.

It is present in everything and is everywhere.
It has no beginning and no end.
It exists in both the tangible and intangible.
It is the formula for all creation.

To acknowledge the Tao,
Is to recognise that we are all interrelated:
Humans to the Earth,
The Earth to the Universe,
The Universe to Matter,
Matter to Humans.

VERSE 26

A Master Teacher can afford to be light in her manner,
Because she is so secure in her intention.

Embrace the passage of each day
By never losing sight of your goal.
Do not get caught up in the latest gossip,
Or participate in distracting conversations.
If you are restless, frustrated or angry,
You have lost touch with your greater purpose.
You are no longer resonating with the Tao.

VERSE 27

A Master Teacher's ability to educate others
Does not rely on how many degrees she has,
Or what university she attended.
The amount of content a teacher knows
Does not equate to how well they will teach it.

A Master Teacher will never pass judgement on her students.
She helps all and cares for them.
She is a facilitator,
There to assist another reach their full potential.

For why be a teacher, if you do not wish to serve others?
The most challenging student makes for the greatest learning.
If you don't understand what the role of the teacher is,
And fail to enjoy every child you work with,
Then you will always be confused,
No matter how intelligent you are.

VERSE 28

A Master Teacher can be proactive,
But knows that true power lies in being passive.
Be like a child and learn again
To watch and observe in appreciation.

Know that when motivation is required,
Wait only until it is inspired.
Inspiration comes from introspection.
If you embrace this pattern of living,
Then you are acting from the Tao.
Not as a doer, but as a creator.

Be involved,
But stay detached.
Experience the world as it is,
Then withdraw to recharge.
Practise self-compassion.

Do not forget to return always to the Tao,
To your state of stillness and calmness
Acquired through meditation or self-reflection.
This way you prepare yourself better
To become a great influencer.

VERSE 29

Do you think you can take over a group of children and truly control them?
It cannot be done.
Each child has their own mind, and their own will.
They are creators, just as you are.

The stronger the force you push onto others,
The stronger the force which will push back against you.

Class dynamics are sensitive.
At times children want to be lead,
At others they want to lead.
At times they want your help,
At others they want independence.
At times they want your attention,
At others they want autonomy.
At times they are energetic,
At others they are withdrawn.

Thus a Master Teachers knows
That an effective leader accepts these dynamics.
She avoids extreme reactions,
Is empathetic and centred.

VERSE 30

A Master Teacher does not rule from the ego.
If a teacher believes that a class needs to be controlled,
They will find that they themselves will be.
For to act with hostility,
Will create further aggression.

A Master Teacher understands that the atmosphere in a class
Must stay open and supportive.
A Master Teacher has no need to be liked,
She does not look for glory nor does she doubt her own abilities.
Her manner is firm, yet yielding.
Her presence is strong, yet supple.
She is powerful without being dominating.
She is interested, but does not interfere.

VERSE 31

*There will be times when force is needed
And penalties handed out.
The Master Teacher uses these tactics
Only sparingly.*

*Punitive action breeds fear
And discourages growth.
The Master Teacher understands that to enhance learning
One needs a calm and supportive environment.
Therefore she will work towards pulling students up,
Rather than pushing them down.
If a rule has been broken,
And harsh punishment must be applied,
It is done so, but reluctantly.
For there may be an immediate victory claimed,
But a long term injury created.
There is no rejoice in knowing
That a child is apologising just to please you,
Rather than because they believe it is right.*

*Long term, a child will become angry and not know why.
Plotting, revenge and retaliation ensues.
The greater the interference from adults,
The less students learn of Nature's law
Of cause and effect.*

VERSE 32

*The energy that creates life
Cannot be defined nor contained.*

*It is smaller than every attempt made to find it,
Yet it is so great as to create whole universes.*

*If every teacher were to live with the Tao in mind,
And taught every student the Way too,
How powerful and harmonious the classroom would be.
Students would feel purposeful,
And teachers, fulfilled.*

*It would not be true to the Tao however
To label and standardise this teaching.
For though the Tao is in all, it cannot be controlled.
It remains elusive but accessible to everyone.
Our choice to travel the Way
Is uniquely ours.*

VERSE 33

Understanding your students is important,
Understanding yourself is vital.

To be a Master Teacher
Means mastering the self.
To be a Master Teacher is to be centred,
To draw strength from your centre.

All that you need to be a Master Teacher
You already have within you.
Those who stay true to who they are
Will never be pulled off course.

VERSE 34

The Tao is so powerful
That it creates all things,
Yet it is silent and peaceful.

Once created, the Tao still does not cease,
It continues to serve by nourishing all creatures.
In return, it stakes no claim or ownership,
Does not want or desire,
Nor prefer one thing over the other.
It simply gives.

The true nature of the Tao is obscure,
But its universal impact cannot be denied.
A Master Teacher aims to serve in much the same way.

VERSE 35

A teacher who lives with the Tao in mind,
Attracts her students.
She is peaceful and content,
Is accepting and open minded.
Students feel safe around her.

Students and teachers can be distracted by
Decorative classrooms and interactive games.
To discuss the Tao and how to live harmoniously with it
Seems too serious and abstract.
There is nothing tangible to study,
There is nothing obvious to listen for.
Yet if tapped into, would be the most powerful lesson ever taught.

VERSE 36

A teacher cannot demand respect
If she is not prepared to give it to others.
The tighter a teacher holds onto the rules,
The more rules will need to be applied.
To have students willingly follow a teacher,
The teacher must first allow free will.

The thoughtful, subtle and gentle manner
Will overcome the hard and aggressive.
The water will eventually wear down the stone.

Just don't reveal your methods,
Let your results speak for themselves.

VERSE 37

To be a good teacher,
Allow yourself to be taught.
The less you do, the more you will be.

If students were able to seek knowledge,
Rather than have it thrust upon them,
How much more productive the classroom would be.
A Master Teacher does not force learning,
But reads the natural rhythms of her students,
As she does so with herself.
Being more kind and taking less action
Accomplishes more.

VERSE 38

*Inspired learning
Needs no teachers.
Informed instruction
Requires education.*

*When teachers work with kindness in mind,
Very little work needs to be done.
When teachers work from a sense of duty,
Much work remains undone.*

*When teachers feel something is lacking,
They do what they think is best to fix it.
But righteous deeds lead to Righteousness,
And honourable feats lead to Honour.
Judging others in the name of Virtue,
Is not virtuous.*

*Enforcing strict rules and rituals
Only serves to lower standards.
Students will only meet you at the point
Where your belief in them lies.*

A Master Teacher does not need
To stress about outcomes.
Because she knows of the Way things work,
She trusts how the process will unfold.
Only the present experience is important,
And the future will follow.

VERSE 39

If you were to look to Nature for inspiration,
You would notice all things work according to unwritten laws:
The sun travels the skies,
The earth is bound by gravity,
The seasons will change,
And the characteristics of leaders whom we admire most,
All work together in harmony as part of a greater whole.

If Nature were to act with the ego in mind,
The sun would come and go as she pleases,
The earth would no longer be grounded,
Seasons would change their order at whim,
And leaders would do only what is best for them.
Chaos would ensue.

A teacher who knows that she does not know everything,
Will act with more compassion and humility.
A teacher who knows she is just a small part of the whole,
Will not feel the need to assert her power or control.

A Master Teacher is successful,
Because she is not driven by her own success.
Her restraint is what helps her
Achieve so much.

VERSE 40

*Gaining more by being independent rather than interdependent
Is an illusion.
Working as groups, within communities,
Is our natural state of being.
At our core, we are all interconnected.
Letting go of the ego, going with the flow,
Is how to move forward exponentially.*

VERSE 41

When wise teachers learn about How things happen,
They will study it and put it into practice.
When average teachers learn about How things happen,
They will consider it, then will forget it.
When foolish teachers learn about How things happen,
They will laugh and call it nonsense,
But there must be foolishness for there to be wisdom.

They laugh because it seems to them that:
The Tao is too obscure and fictitious,
The easiest way forward must be the most difficult,
To take a step back is to admit defeat,
To give is to sacrifice,
To be selfless and kind is a sign of weakness.

VERSE 42

*Remember that every part of what it is to be human
Exists inside both you and each child you teach.
Focus on modelling harmony by embracing all states.*

*To feel a sense of belonging,
Do not fear solitude.
To achieve a sense of control,
Respect chaos.
To speak volumes,
Be silent.
To know balance,
Understand extremes.
Remind children that you can only gain
By letting go.*

*Master Teachers say:
Nature is not forced.
A forceful nature will only result,
In equal forces pushing back.*

VERSE 43

The gentlest personalities can overcome the hardest.
Avoid escalating conflicts by stepping back when needed.

Creating a sense of space relaxes tensions.
It pulls others towards you, out of their rigid opposition.

Calmness, silence, stillness are all powerful tools.
They are unnerving for the aggressive soul.
Master Teachers understand that less is more.

VERSE 44

Ask yourself: what attracted you to teaching?
What is worth more to you: building a reputation or becoming more self-aware?
Is it better to succeed, or is it better to fail?

If you look to others for approval and self-worth,
You will never be satisfied.
The burden you carry will be
The responsibility for another's happiness,
So you will neglect your own.

Once you are content with who you are, what you have, who you teach,
You will feel a sense of overwhelming abundance.
As you begin to appreciate everything that you have,
Anything more will be seen as a bonus.

This is the secret to ongoing happiness.

VERSE 45

Within disorder
There is order.
Within dysfunction
There is function.
Within imperfection
There is perfection.

A Master Teacher understands that
Perception is only skin deep.

Fullness is felt by allowing emptiness.
Riches are attained by owning nothing.
The most profound advice seems so simple.
The greatest impact comes from doing little.

VERSE 46

When a society is in harmony with the Tao,
Curiosity and innovation are signs of successful learning.
When a society is in disharmony with the Tao,
Testing and curriculums are signs of successful education.

Demanding what should be learnt,
And judging this knowledge in a competitive environment,
Reflects the state of a nation
Which has too little faith,
And wants much more control,
Over its own children.

Advancements will only occur
When one allows the mind to roam.

VERSE 47

A Master Teacher does not need
To travel the world to see
Its perfection reflected in the
Faces of all her children.

A Master Teacher does not need
To look out her window,
To appreciate Nature's complex balance,
Revealed in every class she teaches.

The more a teacher searches
For answers beyond the walls
Of her classroom,
The less she will come to understand.

A Master Teacher learns without speaking.
She sees,
Knows,
Understands,
That the lesson is actually for her.

VERSE 48

The true pursuit of knowledge
Is not found in gaining more
But in letting more go.

To understand the Tao
Do less,
And less,
Until a stillness is reached.
That is the point when all knowledge is found.

Master Teachers have learnt to
Stop interfering and to stop pushing back.
For they understand that to master teaching,
Means teaching mastery over self.

VERSE 49

A Master Teacher does not stick to
A stern and inflexible programme.
Instead she remains open to
Responding to the needs of the class.

She cares for the good students,
She cares for the bad.
So that all students can feel they are loved.

She shows confidence in the able students,
She shows confidence in the weak.
So that all students can share in her belief.

A Master Teacher's role is to serve,
And to forget the opinions of others.
Students will naturally test her resolve,
But she will hold steady in her faith and kindness.

VERSE 50

A Master Teacher is not anxious about the future.
She lives in the moment.
She knows that in Nature there is always
An outcome.
Only she can decide to see it as a win or a loss.

A third of her class will
Love success and dread failure.
Another third will
Tolerate failure and prevent success.
And yet another third will
Fear both success and failure.
So almost every student will be spending time
Worrying about what could be,
Rather than what is.

A Master Teacher realises that
Everything will eventually come and go.
That there will always be ups and downs.
Life leads to death,
Death leads to life.
That is how a balanced world works.
So she doesn't spend time trying to control the result,
Nor lets results stop her from living.
That is the greatest lesson she teaches.

VERSE 51

Being in 'the zone'
Is when you are one with the Tao.

The Tao is the life force, the energy
That flows through all people.
When a teacher or student is in harmony with the Tao,
They feel inspired, creative, focused.
When they are one with the Tao,
They are replenished.
When they are one with the Tao,
They are in harmony
With everything around them.

Those who are in 'the zone'
Feel no need to revere the Tao
Or worship it.
This is the same manner in which
A Master Teacher approaches her teaching.
Guide the child to the Tao,
Then take a step back.
Do not take credit.
Do not seek thanks.

VERSE 52

To understand the child
Not only understand the parents,
But understand the Tao too.

The Master Teacher reminds herself daily
Of the origin of all things.
So she remembers that there is so much more
Than just her classroom and her school.

She learns to observe,
Rather than speak.
She learns to be still,
Rather than be busy.
Doing stops her from
Being.

In order to find answers,
One needs patience.
In order to lead with potency,
One needs to know when to yield.

VERSE 53

Being one with the Tao
Requires daily focus.
It is easy to be lead astray
By immediate gratification and
By well-meaning friends and colleagues.

If there is too much concern over prizes and awards,
Then playgrounds are no longer for playing.
If too much money and time is spent on curriculum,
Then classrooms are no longer for learning.
If too much focus is on standardised testing,
Then we don't see the student for the number.
So children and parents become anxious,
And wellbeing programs are implemented.
When all that was needed
Was the way of the Tao.

VERSE 54

A Master Teacher's sense of purpose
Has deep roots.
She will hold steadfast,
And her impact on others
Will be evident generations to come.

If a teacher was in harmony with the Tao,
Her influence would be real.
If a classroom was in harmony,
Its influence would be self-evident.
If a whole school was in harmony,
Its influence would be unmistakable.
If the entire industry was in harmony,
Its influence would know no bounds.

How do I know that these outcomes would happen?
Because I take the time to look.

VERSE 55

Those who are in touch with the Tao
Are like newborn children.
Their bodies are supple and flexible,
Yet their stamina is endless.

They see no distinction between
The feminine and the masculine,
They just feel whole.
They are full of energy,
Being able to last all day and more
Because their source comes from within.

This is how a Master Teacher lives.

Knowing how the world works,
Alleviates any concerns.
Knowing to only focus on the now,
Means always feeling satisfied.
Nature is constantly constant,
Which gives her faith.

VERSE 56

The more a person claims to know,
The less that person actually understands.

Do not engage in gossip.
Block your senses,
Avoid agitation and
Allow the tension to dissipate.

The Master Teacher prefers to sit on the sidelines,
Observing the game from afar.
They will provide advice and guidance,
But will never take sides.
This is what makes them so trustworthy.
A leader for all.

VERSE 57

Being a Master Teacher doesn't mean
Being good at controlling everyone.
She knows that her strength lies in nurturing
Less dependency on the leader.

Controlling all behaviours reduces opportunities for students
To take responsibility for their own actions.
They rely on the enforcement of rules
To determine their self-image and self-worth.

The creation of so many rules
Only serves to reflect
A teacher's own fears and lack of trust.
They stop students from becoming independent,
From becoming honest,
From becoming spontaneous,
From becoming skilled at communicating.

The Master Teacher teaches not by interfering,
But by leading.
She allows others to grow,
By giving them the room to do so.

VERSE 58

If a classroom is run tactfully,
The students won't react with fear.
If a classroom is run carelessly,
The students will only try to push back.

Chasing an ideal classroom
Only serves to make others miserable.
Enforcing strict standards may make
For good behaviour,
But often will rot the goodness out.
Compliance is not respect,
This is what confuses many.

The Master Teacher therefore
Creates boundaries without trapping others,
Is engaged without interfering,
Is straight-talking without judgement,
Is powerful without being overpowering.

VERSE 59

Teachers are leaders,
And leaders demonstrate restraint and control.
Restraint: by reminding oneself that you don't know it all.
Control: by reminding oneself of the Way.

Teachers have limitless ability and influence,
When they decide to see the world as abundant,
And where all is possible.

Being a true leader
Means being firm and fixed
Upon a great vision.

VERSE 60

Dealing with the largest of classes,
Is the same as dealing with one child.
Teach with compassion,
And avoid being overly commanding.

Being one with the Tao
Acknowledges that all emotions will exist,
As will all behaviours.
Allow them all to come and go at their natural pace.
Do not demand a resolution before one is ready,
Or the result may cause more harm than good.

A Master Teacher will not force what is natural,
As what is natural flows.
She knows not add fuel to a fire,
As the fire will eventually burn itself out.

VERSE 61

To be a Master Teacher,
Be like the ocean.
All rivers run to it,
Because it lays low.

The greatest of leaders know
That power 'comes to', it is not 'gained from'.

What may seem at first the least powerful,
Most submissive,
Most passive position,
Is, in fact, the most influential.

For to be able to admit to mistakes,
To be able to point out your own faults,
To have the ability to submit,
Are all signs of one who is in control.

The Master Teacher understands
That her role is to serve, and to be receptive.
She is unafraid of challenging conversations,
As she knows that an open, unbiased approach
Dissolves all disputes.

VERSE 62

The Tao exists in everything.
To those whom we perceive are good,
And to those whom we perceive are bad,
The Tao sees no distinction.

You may believe that others are more powerful,
Because of their rank,
Because they speak well.
Because they are famous,
Because they are rich.
But the Tao, like Nature, is indifferent.

So when a new supervisor comes along,
Or a new leader appointed,
Do not praise or cajole,
Or try too hard to prove yourself.
Instead open their mind to the Way things happen
Through your own actions and thoughts.

VERSE 63

Teaching should not feel like a grind.
Be easy on yourself,
Stop trying so hard.
Appreciate all that you have,
And look forward to the future with anticipation.

Complete the difficult tasks first,
While they are small and easy.
Accomplish the great,
By focusing on the minor first.

The simplest advice,
Is the most challenging to follow.
The clearest instruction,
Is the most difficult to master.

The Master Teacher expects
Aspects of her work to be tricky.
So by not underestimating its complexities,
She does not see it as demanding.

VERSE 64

Just as the fragile can be easily shattered,
And the small can be easily lost,
So too can peace be easily spoilt
If problems are not foreseen.

The Master Teacher learns to predict
And to plan accordingly.
The giant oak once began as a seedling,
The greatest of buildings was once just a brick,
The longest of journeys once began with one step.

As soon an idea is proposed
And a strategy put in place,
The Master Teacher knows to stand back
To avoid obstructing the project.

If she rushes in too early,
She prevents others from learning.
If she tries too hard to control the outcome,
She ruins the pleasure of the discovery.
Instead she demonstrates trust in others
By having faith in the natural progression of things.

VERSE 65

All through history
Those who were enlightened
Never taught others how to be.
Instead they instructed their followers
To live simple lives.

Why are some so difficult to teach?
Students who think they know all the answers
Use cleverness like a weapon
And demand that others agree.

Those who are easy to teach
Declare that they don't know it all,
So are open to every idea and proposal.

Being a Master Teacher is about leading,
So don't try to be too clever,
And don't make your life too complex.
Simplicity provides clarity,
And clarity leads to truth.

VERSE 66

Why is the sea greater
Than a thousand streams?
Because it lies low
And all flow to it.

To teach well
Do not talk down to your students.
Lead with humility
And guide others towards you.

A Master Teacher
Never makes her students feel dominated.

Although a leader amongst others
No one feels ruled.

VERSE 67

Even though the Tao is profound and powerful
Anyone who believes they are both, do not live by it.
Because it is so simple and easy
Few can believe that it is real.

There are three qualities found in Master Teachers:
Compassion, humility and moderation.
Compassion leads to empathy, and empathy
Is what makes you kind.
Humility is found in all great leaders, as it takes courage
To admit to your mistakes.
Moderation causes you to be wholly satisfied
With what you already have.

Why you always feel better from giving
Rather than receiving,
Is because you are acting like the Tao.
You have come to acknowledge
That you are part of a greater whole.
And that is what will sustain you for life.

VERSE 68

If you find yourself in conflict with someone,
Show compassion, not aggression.
Avoid confrontations.
Step back and yield instead.

Develop an ability to stay calm and centred.
Wait for the resistance to dissipate,
Then respectfully step forward
So that no one loses face.

Dealing with people in a way
Which allows all to win,
Is a true skill to master.

VERSE 69

If in conflict with someone
Take the path of least resistance.
It is better to conserve your resources
Then waste them trying to convince others
Of your point of view.

When dealing with anger,
Stay grounded.
Push back without pushing.
Be flexible without attacking.

Underestimating the other
Can be your biggest mistake.
Just seeing them as the enemy
Stops you from nurturing the three qualities:
Compassion, Humility and Moderation.
Therefore you have become the enemy yourself.

VERSE 70

These practices are easy to understand
And easy to implement,
Yet few understand them
And fewer yet practise them.

Master Teachers focus within,
Live simple lives,
And are highly disciplined.

VERSE 71

If you think you know everything,
You actually know nothing,
And so will never attempt to change.
That belief is a contagious disease.

If you can admit that you are not complete,
Then you can accept growth.

Master Teachers know the work is never done.
So she becomes her own physician,
And works to cure her own ailments.

VERSE 72

When students become too bold,
And too familiar in your company,
Disaster will strike.

So while some teachers then react
By being demanding and interfering,
Master Teachers stay grounded.
They don't have need for the praise of their students.
They are confident in their own identity
And know the power of their own presence.
It is in this way that they teach without teaching.

VERSE 73

A teacher who is too brash and fervent,
Can wound others.
A teacher who is too cautious and self-effacing,
Can be unhelpful.
So which is the better way of being?

The Master Teacher is like the Tao,
She lives with ease.
She does not see life as a race,
So always wins.
Does not see the need to command others,
So is always followed.
Does not appear ambitious,
Yet is the most successful.

VERSE 74

If all students were taught to remain observant,
And took their life lessons from Nature,
They would soon realise not to fear change.
For to do so is pointless,
And to deny it, impossible.

The anxious student tries to control the future.
So like an apprentice using her master's tools,
She harms herself needlessly.

VERSE 75

*Students become rebellious
When there are too many rules.
Students stop learning
When there are too many demands.
When schools start reacting to the needs of adults rather than children,
They soon lose the meaning of their own existence.*

*Loosen the grips of control and fear.
Trust in a child's ability to learn and grow.*

VERSE 76

The younger the child,
The easier they can be trained and guided.
Like a newly emerged seedling,
They are supple and pliable,
So don't expect rigidity.

The older the tree,
The more brittle it becomes.
So when winds of change come
And blow a gale, as they will,
Those who can bend and yield will survive.
Those who are hard and resistant will crack.

Keep your nature soft,
And your approach to life, fresh.

VERSE 77

Consider the way an archer's bow responds
When the string is pulled:
Top lowers to meet bottom,
Bottom rises to meet top.
Where power is in excess, it is drawn upon.
Where it is depleted, it is replenished.

When the string is released,
And pressure is eased,
The bow returns to its original state.
This is how the Tao works:
It will always seek to restore balance.

Those who are not in touch with the Tao,
See scarcity when tension arises.
They become anxious,
Hold on tighter,
And look to restore control.

The Master Teacher understands
That there is never any shortage.
Life is cyclical,
What has once been will come again.

She fears no change,
Willingly imparts all her knowledge,
Openly shares all her resources,
Is generous with her time,
And does not give in to stressful times.

VERSE 78

Water is both at once
The softest yet most powerful element in the world.
It immediately gives way to any obstacle,
But can wear down even the hardest rock over time.

So this is what Master Teachers learn:
Time and focus are our greatest assets.
Yet why do so few of us use them?

Be humble enough to submit to others,
And you will end up leading them.
Be single-minded in your efforts,
And you will gain the world's attention.

The paradoxical truth:
You will gain more by doing less.

VERSE 79

Everyone wants to work towards solving a problem,
But if you carry on complaining and resenting
Even after a solution has been found,
Then what is the point of reconciling?

A Master Teacher knows that it is more important,
In order to make herself feel better,
To demonstrate compassion,
Rather than demand it of others.

To give is to serve.
To command is to take.

VERSE 80

If schools were kept small, and classes smaller,
There would be no need for the latest gimmicks,
As children would already have all that they need
For successful learning.

Students can be given the most advanced technology,
And have access to the smartest teachers,
But if you fail to show interest in them,
Then they will lose interest in learning.

If quality time was prioritised
With mentors as well as with peers,
Greater would the impact be
Of schools and of teachers.
For students can know content,
Rote-learn their facts and figures,
But it is from human interaction,
That they learn what it is to be human.

VERSE 81

The truth is always blunt.
Never polished.
That is what lies are for.
Master Teachers do not demand others to agree,
Those who argue only serve to reinforce their own limited views.

If we insist on teaching students to express themselves clearly,
Then we must ensure they learn to listen just as eloquently.

The Master Teacher knows she does not know it all,
She does not hold on to one way of doing things,
She stays malleable, adaptable,
Always seeks to learn more.
She is giving and selfless,
Taking pains to share every lesson she has learnt.
Through these deliberate actions she says to the world:
There is an abundance of knowledge out there!
And knowledge of abundance as well.
In essence, her success lies in striving to become The Teacher,
Rather than perfecting teaching itself.

www.ingramcontent.com/pod-product-compliance
Lightning Source LLC
Chambersburg PA
CBHW050320010526
44107CB00055B/2329